Coming Out of Nowhere

Homestead house

Potter Highway
(now called the Old Seward Highway)

Alaska Railroad

O'Malley Road

An aerial photo taken in 1950 that shows the location of the
homestead south of Anchorage. (Photo © Quantum Spatial)

Coming Out of Nowhere

ALASKA HOMESTEAD POEMS

Linda Schandelmeier

University of Alaska Press • Fairbanks

Text © 2018 Linda Schandelmeier

Published by
University of Alaska Press
P.O. Box 756240
Fairbanks, AK 99775-6240

Cover design by UA Press.
Interior design by Kristina Kachele.

Photographs in the book are from the Schandelmeier family collection, unless otherwise noted.

Cover image: Linda Schandelmeier stands in front of her family's new 1959 Chevy station wagon purchased with some of the receipts from selling part of the homestead (1959).

Section One: Linda's mother loads peat to sell to help make ends meet (ca. 1955).

Section Two: Linda's sister (right) and Linda could find amusement even on a pile of logs (ca. 1951–52).

Section Three: Linda's brother (right) and Linda snowshoe on the homestead. Common winter activities were ice skating, snowshoeing, and skiing (1959–60).

Section Four: Linda attended the University of Alaska in Fairbanks and earned a degree in biological sciences in 1971 (ca. 1968).

Names: Schandelmeier, Linda, 1949–author.
Title: Coming out of nowhere : Alaska homestead poems / by Linda
    Schandelmeier.
Other titles: Alaska homestead memoir : poems
Description: Fairbanks, AK : University of Alaska Press, 2018. |
Identifiers: LCCN 2017059959 (print) | LCCN 2018002640 (ebook) | ISBN
    9781602233614 (e-book) | ISBN 9781602233607 (pbk. : alk. paper)
Subjects: LCSH: Schandelmeier, Linda , 1949– | Poets, American—Biography. |
    Home—Alaska—Poetry. | Frontier and pioneer life—Alaska—Poetry. |
    Alaska—Poetry.
Classification: LCC PS3619.C32575 (ebook) | LCC PS3619.C32575 A6 2018 (print)
    | DDC 811/.6--dc23
LC record available at https://lccn.loc.gov/2017059959

*For my parents, Nell and John Schandelmeier, and my sister
and brother, Jeanette and John, who lived on the homestead,
and for my husband, John Davies, whose steadfast love and
support and insightful comments made this a better book.*

CONTENTS

Looking up O'malley '51

Looking east up the unpaved and sparsely populated O'Malley Road in 1951 (Pastro family collection).

The homestead house was made of framing lumber, and the garage was built from local spruce logs (ca. 1951–52).

PREFACE

Even though the homestead lay just six miles south of the fledg-ling town of Anchorage, Alaska, there was no road access when my father filed for the land in 1946. To reach the property, he parked on the often muddy Campbell Creek Trail, which branched off Campbell Creek Road (Potter Drive on today's maps), and walked about two miles south along the railroad tracks and then a quarter of a mile east across a low-lying area of black spruce. The home-stead—legally described as Seward Meridian, Alaska, T. 12 N., R. 3 W., Section 20, NW ¼ NW ¼; Section 17, N ½ SW ¼ & SW ¼ SW ¼— was L-shaped along the east side of the Old Seward Highway, with 120 acres north of O'Malley Road and 40 acres to the south.

Our frame cabin stood in a small clearing about a hundred yards from the west boundary of the homestead. The Seward Highway (now called the Old Seward Highway), provided access from Anchorage and was constructed to the Rabbit Creek area in the fall of 1947. When the road was originally built it was called Potter Highway, or sometimes Potter Road.

My father, who arrived from Arizona in 1940 as a twenty-three-year-old, often said moving to Alaska was the best decision he ever made. My mother came to Anchorage when she was in her early twenties, after spending a year at the University of Alaska in Fairbanks. The two of them met at the Lido Hotel and Café in Anchorage and married in 1947. Mom was no stranger to hard work, having grown up in the Alaska coastal town of Seldovia, where her family built their own boats and fished for salmon.

Meanwhile, Anchorage, incorporated in 1920, was experiencing rapid growth that was fueled by World War II and the construction,

My parents met at Anchorage's Lido Hotel and Café
(on Fourth and B Streets). The cafe was rebuilt after the
1964 earthquake but later destroyed by fire (ca. 1946–50).

beginning in 1940, of Fort Richardson army base. Many people,
including my father, found work related to the military buildup.
The 1950 census listed the population of Anchorage as 11,254,
more than three times larger than the 1940 census. By 1960, 44,397
people called this area home.

In spite of the changes brought on by rapid growth, many home-
steaders lived as they always had. To acquire title to their land they
needed to meet the requirements of the Homestead Act: file an
application, improve the land—or "prove up" as it was called—and
file for a deed of title. Proving up involved clearing land for a dwell-
ing and for agricultural purposes, building a house (at least twelve
by fourteen feet in size) that was your primary residence, living
on the land for five years, and cultivating ten acres. The physical
labor entailed to satisfy these requirements was demanding, and
homesteaders often needed other jobs to raise money for necessi-
ties even after they acquired the patent to their land from the U.S.
Bureau of Land Management Patent Office.

Moose and caribou that could readily be hunted formed a large
part of our staples, along with local crops. We grew potatoes and
raised chickens for meat and eggs. Canned milk and vegetables
rounded out the rest of our diet.

Dad works on the roof of the homestead house (1947).

Dad hung moose meat in the doorway of the garage in preparation for skinning and butchering (ca. 1957).

My sister (middle) and I (right) talk to a field hand in the potato field located on the lower forty acres of the homestead, south of O'Malley Road and east of the Old Seward Highway (ca. 1955–58).

Money was tight and not always available. School supplies, clothing, and rare extras took careful budgeting. We wore hand-me-downs and learned to take good care of them and of our other possessions. Wet shoes meant a spanking. Food was served at mealtime, and no one thought of raiding the cookie stash during the day. Mom was the chief accountant and budget overseer.

Meandering through the surrounding forests in search of adventure was a major pastime, along with reading. We looked forward to our weekly trip to town, which usually included a chance to check out books at the Z. J. Loussac Public Library.

Our family earned a living growing potatoes for most of a decade. Dad and Mom also sold topsoil and peat and later gravel from a pit located on the homestead. Mom loaded peat, graded potatoes, and chopped wood, on top of doing most of the household chores and childcare. My younger brother John, my older sister Jeanette, and I were best playmates, roaming the homestead on foot in summer

Homesteaders rarely took pictures, and when they did, it was usually when someone was dressed up for school or church. This was probably the first day of school, in 1957, when my brother (left), my sister (right), and I posed for this shot.

and on skis and snowshoes in winter. You could say it was an insular existence. Make-believe, a deck of cards, and the outdoors happily occupied us. We didn't know any other life, except what we glimpsed in the chatter of our classmates at school. Swimming lessons, birthday parties, and books from the school book order were for others.

As Anchorage spread south, homesteads were subdivided and sold, and the old lifestyle began to disappear. Part of our homestead was sold in 1959, with the remaining few acres that included the old house and garage gone by 2002. If the homestead existed in its entirety today, it would be bordered on the west by the Old Seward Highway and extend south from East 100th Avenue across O'Malley Road to O'Malley Centre Drive. The trees and open land have been replaced with a maze of streets, condos, and businesses.

The poems in this book are based on my memories and experiences growing up on this homestead. Because poems are not journalistic endeavors, they often tell the "truth" in a way that may not be straightforward. The way of poets, as Emily Dickinson described in her poem #1129, is to "Tell all the Truth but tell it slant—." These poems sometimes take a circuitous route in order to arrive at a deeper truth.

One

COUNTRY OF STRANGERS

Seward Meridian, Alaska, 1950s

A coin tossed on a table top in Bisbee, Arizona. Heads or tails, my buddy said. Panama or Alaska? I wasn't looking for meaning. Just putting distance between me and the copper mines, their bitter underground. You don't worship anything here, just out-run the echoes following you. In Alaska 160 acres of homestead land is free. An ax, a field. A rifle, meat. Trees string their green over the landscape. It comes off on your skin. I met a woman at the Lido Hotel bar who looked like a movie star. Her green eyes held a history I thought I could talk her out of. A man and a woman make a duet. People pay for potatoes we grow, gravel and peat we dig. I'm not planning to come up empty. That dot in the forest is our cabin, lumber piled under tarps. Our daughter watches swallows swoop and dive above our clearing. She says they turn the air violet-green with their wings.

DRIVING BY THE OLD HOMESTEAD

I've pulled off the road to stare
at the homestead. I forget my manners,
gawk at the nothing remaining
of our house and garage,
the forests.
What did I inherit from walks
in the deep woods, from watching wind sway
the bluejoint grasses?
Even digging in the yard
all you would find is ashes.

I'd be called a stranger by anyone
watching me,
but I can tell you
what it was like before roads—
when my father in his khaki shirt
and pants hiked the railroad tracks
hauling supplies,
crossed the swamp to this land.
And my mother split kindling
for the wood stove every morning.
About my sister and her pigeons,
my brother's metal boat.
We thought it was our place,
our childhood.

Now familiar mountains
on the skyline slip out of clouds,
gossip pink and purple.
Their colors cut me,
the only thing I recognize—
unexpected, like an injury.

I am the girl who grew up here.
This is my place,
where memory began.

MOUNTAINS LIKE RIBS

From the tiny tarpapered house,
the pigeon and chicken coops,
the unpeeled spruce log garage
chinked with moss,
the tin-roofed woodshed—
we could see the mountains
holding up the sky.
They kept us alive—
we believed that like religion.

The three of us,
two girls and a boy,
ran out along footpaths
and imagined mountains
like ribs circling our hearts.
We found bluebells
and yarrow, bleached white,
wandered into swamps
where sundew dissolved
insects—their leaves like slow tongues.

Dust from the fields in our hair,
chips of wood
on our clothes from stoking the stove.
In the house, uncovered insulation.
In our bellies
canned milk, potatoes, moose meat.

Mother rubbing our shirts on a washboard,
feeding the wringer washer,
clipping laundry to clotheslines
her face stiff, hands tired.

Father plowing fields,
driving the loader back and forth
hauling stones for the gravel trucks
until evening when he closed his eyes
the newspaper spread over his face.

Mountains watched over us
as we slept soundly
not hearing the night in the trees,
which were friendly beings,
their rattling leaves
like lullabies in the wind.

My father lashed us daily with a hose,
bruises on our bodies
like berry stains.
When he drank we'd tiptoe
through the hours he was home.
He'd slap my mother,
and even my baby sister, Rose.
I learned to hide there,
taught that to my kids,
a good skill to know.

The homestead where I live now
is miles from Seldovia, far from my father
whose epitaph will be:
"Here lies a mean man,
a fisherman, a drunk."
With the caterpillar tractor, I load peat
from the swamp. My dark, unruly curls
tucked under a red bandana.
I mend our clothes, patch holes,
sew on buttons, manage the finances,
chop spruce or birch for the stove.

As a kid
I peddled cabbage and carrots we grew,
hauled them around town in a wagon,
sold milk from our cow,
my little finger still crooked
from carrying crates of bottles.
They'd buy from a girl,
not from my brothers who cheated them.

Now we have a bank loan
for the root cellar.
The payments beckon like a pit
we might step into any month.
The children know not to ask for anything,
not even what money can't buy.
Maybe they learned from me
wanting leads to heartache.

In Seldovia, I'd walk the path
along the slough to town,
look out at the water changing color,
gray or blue, flecked with foam.
In winter, its inshore shallows scoured by ice.
Like our homestead, it was beautiful, remote;
houses built along the water,
instead of in pockets of trees.
Rafts of black and silver ducks rode the swells.
Masts of the fishing boats in the harbor
reached toward the canopy of clouds.

TODAY IS ALL THEY HAVE

When my uncle drives up on his new motorcycle
we run outside and gawk
while he grins, revs the engine
rides the concrete walkway
around the house.

He muscles that machine
through the tight turns,
then stops in front, kickstand down.
Sun collects in the folds of his leather jacket
his black hair combed back in waves like Fabian.

He pulls a nickel from behind my brother's ear
and steals my nose.
We wonder what Mom will say
about these shenanigans,
but she is smiling.

They laugh together—
the silhouette their arms take
as they talk, the easy movements.
She doesn't know that today is all they have
the yard steeped in light.

He was five when their mother
was sent to an asylum.
As the ship left the dock
they held their arms tight against their sides
keeping embraces they couldn't give.

On the nearby pilings cormorants waited,
their black feathers like cloaks,
their shapes lit by morning's haze—
silent, looking out for fish.

Years later, in the local newspaper
she reads that pieces of his fishing boat
washed up on that same beach,
his body worn out by water,
never found.

In her dreams he's a gray gull,
feathers flattened by wind,
the curve of its wing like an arch
they could walk through to safety.

BAKING LESSONS

My mother
loads the wood stove,
lights the fire—
shows me

how to sift flour,
cream margarine and sugar.
How to crack eggs,
keep shells out of the batter.

This room is crowded
with her corrections,
and her leftover wishes.

Heaps of words, yesterday
and before.

MOMMA SAID

Momma said, leave
when you turn eighteen—

I can't own you then.

You'll come back
opinionated, mouthy.

But right now
I control you.

You have no voice.

Growing up is a fire
I can't put out.

See how our family burns.

I douse you girls
with water,

protect you when I can.

THE WINTER MEAT

Frost bristles the low grass,
leaves on the ground harden,
as I shoulder my rifle,
hike the trail to the plywood platform
set high in a spindle of branches
above the swamp where moose fatten
on summer-sweetened plants.
Hunger hovers close,
stares from the half-lit trees.
Some evenings, I'm lucky,
and one slips into the clearing,
lowers his head toward the peaty soil.
We need the meat, will use all of it—
the heart and tongue boiled and sliced
for sandwiches. The liver and kidneys
fried for other meals.
From their swings in the yard
the kids listen
for the crack of my rifle,
while bleached antlers from past hunts
wait like wordless petitions
on our woodshed roof.

MY FATHER HILLING POTATOES

I loved my father that day
watching him hill potatoes
with the red tractor,
his brown khaki cap tilted
to shade his eyes.
If I told him,
I would give something up,
no longer kept invisible
by the grace of silence.
I chose to stay in the willow's shadows
as he drove up and down
the rows of plants,
their open blossoms
spilling white across the field.

Two

GIRL MADE OF FOG

From the archives of one whose first word
was snow, whose hands don't remember maps.

This is just an intermission in the long glide called leaving. In
the middle of my childhood, bird's voices like broken bells coiled
around my dawn. I was stranded by indifferent siblings, mind fog
entered spaces in my head. I shut my mouth, only let in words from
books. Still I understood little. What about the sharpening stone
like the wheel of a bicycle on a wooden stand turned by peddling—
overgrown by weeds? The drum of Premerge weed killer staining
the dirt garage floor yellow, voles under stacked pallets asking
not to be poisoned? I preferred stands of birch or scrawny spruce.
These whose roots wandered peaty soil, shaped slow sugar in their
veins at night. I noticed their bark, lenticels, petioles, bone-colored
branches. Like a bible written in hieroglyphics, they had words, if I
could read them.

SUMMER UNTETHERED

I head south, cross the muskeg,
step carefully around the wettest areas
trying to keep my shoes dry.
Time for blooming—
yellow marsh marigolds
and fuzzy catkins of Sitka Burnet
unfold their flowers, draw me in
until I'm barely human.
I banish mosquitoes by waving
a willow branch around my head.
The day is clouds, a bit of sun.
Not many cars on O'Malley Road,
so I break the rule about crossing it
and head farther south
toward the root cellar and potato field.
Black spruce trees keep talking,
change shape,
come back again as crows.
I pay them no mind.
When I drift out at the edge of the forest
it is almost dinnertime
and my shoes are wet.
I powder them dry with fine gray ash
saved from the last Mount Spurr eruption
to avoid a beating from Mama's ruler.
Before I go inside
I take one more drink of sweet air.

HUM

of mosquitoes,
our bodies in the crosshairs.

How used
to their buzzing we are—

but summer's leaves
unfolding like a green fan

are never ordinary—
nor June's sun, warm on our skin

or a kingfisher's clattering call
echoing in the river trees.

LEDA

To have nothing but this—
a yard, and a gander.

This place
with its sagging spruce pole fence
and muddy path, his realm.

Breathing wild roses, I pick up a stick
when I hear his territorial honking.

This is my world,
pushed back from the road—
the sky's blue roof,
mountains like a saw blade.

In the nearby grass
a white-crowned sparrow trills
his mating song.

Then he saunters into view,
hooligan orange feet and hostile blue eyes.
He runs at me hissing.

I grab him, wrap white wings
tight against his body,
and with the other hand,
hold his swan-like neck and beak away.

I deposit him squawking
inside the chicken yard.

He ruffles his feathers—
still king of the grounds.

For now, we are even.
An unreliable peace
floats like willow cotton over the afternoon.

HORSE CALLED CHARLIE

I thought of riding
the strawberry roan,

imagined
I was part antelope or centaur,

the mirage of us bareback—

lost in the bright bloom
of childhood.

He was swaybacked, jittery.

Staked in a muddy field
he'd escape into the loud world
outside his fence.

I tired of bringing him back
to the brown pasture

where he was diminished,
dwarfed by
my expectations.

All he wanted was to graze
on the wild, sweet grass

that grew along the road.

ALONG THE PRINT

Grass-of-Parnassus grow along the path to our swamp,
their waxy petals like stars
bursting white above the black mud,
and narrow petals of yellow flowers
we call peanut butters,
never learning their real name.

Footprints of night creatures linger in the soft earth—
a record of those who passed unseen
so close to our place.
Rocks form stepping-stones
to my sister's boarding house
where I build a room without a roof,
furnish it with a rug of horsetail.
My brother plays the superhero
slashing at us with his willow-branch sword.

I can't see tomorrow following me—
we are children, not carrying coats or coins
or memories yet.
We still believe the black spruce
are lords of everything.

SLEEPWALKING TOWARD MYSELF

The day our next-door neighbor took us to Turnagain Track,
the sun hung in the sky like a lemon drop.
My skin was warm,
the sun's touch sweet.

Leaning toward the oval track,
eating Cracker Jacks
someone else bought, was that okay?
My parents wouldn't spend money like this.

Cars drove in circles, their engines
roaring like beasts from fairy tales.
Their bodies slipped by each other
like metal eels trying not to touch.

The noise was long, I sucked in
the acrid smell of rubber,
the particles of dust.
Who knew I might love this?

I went into the afternoon
sleepwalking toward myself,
never knowing who our neighbor was,
never imagining he was kind.

STEALING THE STRAWBERRIES

Our neighbor watches us
scramble across the drainage ditch

that divides our properties.
Two girls and a boy who skirt the forest edge,

stoop small, trying to blend
in to the backdrop of green winglike boughs.

He smiles as we sprint over shorn grass
toward his strawberry patch,

remembering childhood double-dares
sliding under barbed wire,

lifting buddies over fences to filch apples.
Not supposed to be in his yard,

still we leap toward what is not ours,
paint ourselves invisible in our minds.

The world is loud footfalls and heartbeats
as we slip past the glassy eyes of his house.

The strawberries are ripe now
and impossibly sweet.

NO ONE ASKS ABOUT THE BRIDGE

Charlie, our packhorse, is tied in the pasture
nosing wild grass like he's never been away,
belly full of our potatoes.

Before that there was no time to dally.
It was a relief no one was around
except the rooster crowing down by the house.

Before that everything was topsy-turvy, wrecked—
even alders in the ditch with their branches
and toothed leaves reminded me of past whippings
for broken dishes and wet shoes.

Before that I chose the shortcut
over our small footbridge
nailed together from skinny spruce and planks.
Partway across, poles splintered,
sagged V-shaped toward the ditch,
dangled midair as we skittered to safe ground.

Before that, big as a moose, Charlie followed me—
if he bolted, I might have been dragged
through Jonesy's field, tangled in willows
and sharp stalks of dry grass.

Before that I grabbed the frayed rope
hanging like a serpent from his neck,
hoped the pail of culled potatoes I carried
would tempt him home.

Before that I set out to catch him.
I was almost ten,
I knew to lure him in
by rattling the pail of food.

Before that I noticed that Charlie
had broken free from his stake
in the muddy ground.

Before that small tufts of wind stirred
the quaking aspen leaves.
It was a perfect June day, juncos fussing
in last year's leaves,
their black-and-white tails like fans.
The sun playing peek-a-boo
in the shredded summer clouds.

IN THE PLAYHOUSE

First time ever
the neighbor boy

shows up like a spook

walking up the driveway,
so quiet even the chickens

don't twitch.

He's thin with straight sandy-red hair
the color of wild grass tops.

I think he's exotic,
but maybe any boy
besides my brother

is exotic.

In the playhouse
he sits opposite me—

I serve animal crackers
and milk.

A trellis of shadows
climbs the wall behind us
as we stare out the window
at the mountains.

I don't say that I saw him
looking at me on the school bus,

he doesn't tell me
his family is moving next week

and this is his farewell.

SLEEPING THE CHICKENS

If you come upon the house,
miles from the city,
you might see children
making their own amusement
by tucking chickens' heads under their wings,
then swinging them side to side
like the motion of a clock's pendulum.
Over and over they do this
until the birds are still, eyes closed.
Each hypnotized body placed
on its side in the yard.
They sleep, still as rocks,
unless someone startles them awake—
their multihued feathers like confetti
in the summer grass.

CHILDHOOD, SWALLOW

A sliver of light from the door,
        she enters the dark garage.

Wings thrash
        against the window,
a blue-green swallow trapped
        against the mirrored sky.

Branches of trees, their black trunks,
        reflect on the glass.

The world is hushed.

She cups its iridescent feathers
        in her hands,
looks into its eyes.

        The bird is fierce,
like the sky is in her,
        the storm,
the lightning.
        She knows she has to let it go.

ICE'S APPRENTICE

This is how the cold knows her—
each stroke and glide of her skates,
each ice crystal

claiming her toes
as she circles the small pond.
She's an Olympic skater
coached by winter.

Home from school
after the hour bus ride,
she shovels her own rink.

Dusk writes on her slate of ice.
Its lead-gray pencil
rubs over her whole sky.

DECEMBER'S TREE

We shuffle our path,
snowshoes stiff,
sky winter gray,
clouds calling snow.

Already
the snowquiet's spell
inside us.

Now the season's tree
circled by our tracks.
We cut it,
tow it home.

Three

This was almost the worst year of my life. It was before man walked
on the moon. We lived among wild trees. I needed deodorant but
was afraid to say so. This was before my parents mentioned body
odor, menstruation, or sex. They were divorced. I was still dream-
ing of being popular. Watergate was years away. No mass transit
buses or car I could drive, no boyfriend. Not before my mom said
when you turn eighteen, I'll break your plate. She'd already made a
career of suffering. I wasn't planning on following in her footsteps.
You've already guessed women's lib and birth control weren't top-
ics in our house. No one was home except me, so I slipped out to the
road, my babysitting money in my cutoff jeans pocket, stuck my
thumb out, caught a ride on the back of a stranger's Harley. Burned
the inside of my knee on the muffler. It was a price I didn't mind
paying. I was keeping an appointment with the rest of my life.

PAINTING THE STONES

Opening the door
to the chicken house
I discover him
stiff and bloodied on the coop floor.

So quiet
I could hear the wind outside.
It seemed unearthly.
I felt a jolt against my ribs
as if something inside me
had shifted.
The other roosters acted like nothing
had happened.

I'd raised him from a chick,
called him Goldy,
his pumpkin-colored feathers
edged in black
so it looked like he wore a lace coat
as he scratched up bugs
in the dirt for the hens.

I didn't want to touch him,
his strut and verve drained away—
wanted to be remote,
not a coroner, mortician
preacher, gravedigger.

I wrapped his body in burlap
from a feed sack,
dug a hole,
threw in handfuls of fireweed blossoms

loud and magenta,
marked his grave with colored stones
painted from my watercolor box.

They were a eulogy
I didn't say aloud
because now death had my address.

THE BUTTON BOX

I slip the cardboard box
from the treadle sewing machine drawer.

Snooping they would call it,
but without nearby relatives, family albums,

there's no other entry
into my parents' histories.

So, I lift the hinged lid
of Grandpa's old cigar box

letters, pictures—I imagined those
and jewels maybe,

but it holds only buttons.
Buttons so vivid, the colors

separate me from this drab house
between forest and road.

Explosions of aquamarine, cinnamon,
mulberry, cerulean, vermillion, plum.

I scoop them up, pour them
back and forth between my hands,

listen as they murmur
like water over rocks,

gossip about the shirts
they've opened and closed,

my parents who wore them,
waltzing in moonlight so silver

it made a sound.
Dad's many pledges.

It was an easy vocabulary without hindrances,
but a trick of moonlight.

Unfinished insulation in the passageway,
a plywood floor riddled with knotholes,

the army surplus blankets
on our beds.

Disappointments everywhere,
even the yard—weeds and mud.

Disheveled coops
built from exhausted pallets.

His talk of how he'd bid
on carpet for the living room

at the next surplus sale—
how he'd plant a hedge

of wild cinquefoil,
dug from the forest.

As if they had carpet
or he dug up anything.

As if there was any money,
any will.

He kept up his talk,
his face earnest,

his plans so convincing
I hunted for hope in his words.

I vowed never to live with anyone
capable of so much distortion again,

or in a place
with so many unkept promises

that I tried to keep
when I grew up—

even though they were not my promises,
not my bright unfinished things.

ABOVE THE GARAGE

Summer, I climb wooden steps
with my brother and sister
to the room under the eaves.
Easy in our skin, time doesn't gallop
through the days yet.

We snoop in the hired man's barren room.
His metal lamp without a shade,
single mattress hugging the wall.
Unprepared for his pinups of women,
full red lips twisted into smiles,
huge breasts not like any we know,
but offered to anyone looking.

Outside the room, the unlit alcove
camouflages us,
as we pretend to discover 78-rpm records,
old letters in Italian from Mom's suitcase—
things we've already seen.
Our flashlights whisper
through trunks and boxes stored there,
hide the strangers we've become.

What we know about each other
pulled apart like a garment sewed wrong.
No one knows we are up here,
the undertow of sex on our skin—
as the yard below slumbers.

THE CARD SHARK

He shuffles
the red-and-white deck, deals.

His eyes own this table,
lips curled in a smirk.
It's all attitude.

I know to hold my cards close,
folded together
so no one can see them.

Our words pivot and wheel
until they are all bluff.

He plays as if his life depends on it,
and maybe it does.

Maybe inside
something's cutting him
into ribbons.

Outside the window
cars and trucks move
along the Seward Highway,

but we are in this kitchen
looking out at gray sky.
Rain shellacs our windows,

soaks the garage.
The summer we are hungry for
shanghaied by rain.

We play rummy, cribbage,
compare our hands,
and he keeps beating me.

I do not consider
that he might be cheating,

that I have already lost
more than these card games.

BECAUSE MUSIC IS GREEN

When she twirled
in the black-and-red-plaid dress,
hugging her arms tight
against her spinning body
she wasn't my sister.

I could tell the dress sang to her—
her eyes darkened,
as if she was listening to secrets.
I didn't like it.
She was older and already too bossy.

When I put the dress on
there was no music.
Instead the skirt slackened
against my hips, turned me mousy.

I hung it in my closet,
went outside
and climbed the wooden ladder
to the shed roof.

Forests stretched every which way,
willow, spruce,
birch, and aspen.
At the time, I was blind
to all their green music—
how they wore it.

NEIGHBORS

Last night through the screen of trees
I saw their squat one-room cabin as it was,
ghost of the spruce that formed it,
not clinging to the land,
but shaped of dreams and air.

I thought of the family,
the father in overalls, sipping coffee
letting the morning take its shape around him
while his ill-mannered goats
wandered into our yard
and rode our surplus lumber piles
into the creek outside our house.

The mother bunching faded blossoms
on her housedress in her hands,
while her children dressed behind partitions
of boxes, and grain sacks hung for curtains.

Their unplanted fields grew up in saplings
until one evening they were gone
vanished into the quiet air.
Where their cabin stood
trees stretch out their hands
leaning their bodies against the sky.

THE EARTH IS BREAKABLE
(Good Friday Earthquake, March 1964, 9.2 on the Richter scale)

This house, not a house,
but a boat I rock in, my hands
the oars I brace with
as the floor heaves and rolls
so even the grace of standing
requires a doorway.

My father's birthday cake,
the coffee pot, encyclopedias
tumble toward the rolling floor.
Each one caught
by outstretched hands.
Lights blink out, the radio spits static.
There is no emergency exit.

Outside, telephone wires swing
back and forth like jump ropes,
silver lines glinting
against the black-green spruce
bending like yogis toward the ground
and straightening up.

No school the next morning, loss unfolding
on the radio, I snowshoe
over the March snow crust breached by cracks,
expecting the ground to stir, slash open.
When I throw my voice into fissures
beyond light's reach, only my own vertigo
rises to meet me.

Because the house is intact,
I believe we've escaped damage.
My father stashes his ball in the car,
imagines his bowling league
will meet that night, even as he drives
toward the buckled, impassable road.

I WATCH THE HIRED MEN PICK POTATOES

In the blanched light of morning,
birch trees play their yellow cards,
poking the sky with empty branches.
The hired men drag burlap sacks
over the dug-up field
gathering the round tubers.
Bulging sacks are piled high
on the truck's flatbed as it rattles by.
I keep to myself until lunchtime
when the pickers come to our table
peacock friendly, brandishing their black pails.
I wither against the wall listening,
keeping back from their maleness.
The hour blooms with their talk.
Later, one takes me on fossil-hunting trips,
flashing his schizophrenic smile
before he undresses me.
His love is a knife
he cuts me with.
I make myself empty
until amnesia floats over the day.
I remember only the bearberries' serrated
red leaves, how they scorch and flare.
Around our empty field
the nude trees turn to ice.

OUR FATHER LEAVING US

Out the window I watch you
load shirts gathered from the closet
into your car,
clasping them to your chest
before piling them into the back seat.

Earlier that week you came
into our room to say you were going.
My sister and I could not look at you.
We went on brushing our hair, counting the strokes,
went on learning that Father

is another name
for shadow, for loneliness,
which might meet us
coming home from school,
or out in the yard
where gray trees stand still,

their branches
fracturing the sky,
and sparrows living in the weeds
are silent
as I hear your car engine catch
in the driveway.

NIGHT SOUNDS

All the night sounds bleed
into my clothes
as I loosen the bedroom window
and slide barefoot to the gravel.

Along the path to your trailer
pigeons coo in the lofts,
fireweed gone through burning
shed their sticky seed on my jeans.

Inside you take off my clothes,
each piece removed like skin,
exposing something deeper
than the body.

I was fourteen when you
shoved through the door of our house,
took my shirt apart
unlatching the buttons with your hands.

At first, I washed
put my fingers where you were,
knowing only the power
of tangling a man.

Until there was nothing left to imagine,
waking to the same stiff rooms,
mountains like a wall
slamming into my face,
your shadow always about the place.
I told you to keep away.

Twenty years later
I can do anything but love.
Each man has your body,
I pull them down doing what I learned early.

I was a boy
       when he took me
up the mountain.
       We landed in his plane
on the hillside.
       Walked, exploring,
found geodes
       their cracked interiors
crazed with gems.
       Then he told me
I could pay him for this—
       the fuel for the plane.
He said my body would be enough.
       Whenever he asked for more
I would give it to him.
       Now his letters burned,
ashes scattered,
       I still remember
how he pushed me down
       on the rocks,
pulled off my clothes.
       How sky tilted above us,
and I heard the trees,
       their leaves like tongues
clicking in the wind.

SOMEONE SHOULD HAVE KICKED
THE PEDOPHILES OFF OUR PLACE

I remember how we unraveled
after the men
parked trailers in our clearing.
What did we own to understand their eyes,
the unstalled weather of their longing?

The body does not choose frost
or ice for its doors. It wants
to slide out windows,
believe that stars
are wayposts spilling light.

Night is a shingled roof
above the path pebbled
with footprints
which leads to him
waiting. Who is to tell her
what she will find?
That her parents will not mend her?

Four

TOWER BELLS

Bells rang from the campus water tower, a haunting sound, but welcoming. The kind of sound that holds a message for you. Next, insomnia and I stumbled into glass doors, and I quit God because he didn't allow dancing. In the empty field grown up with saplings, larks landed. Like me they had just arrived from the south to this place of rivers. Foreign ones wondering if they would belong. I was hired at the library because of books. At the time, I thought it was because books were saviors. I owned only two pairs of pants, somehow that meant I didn't know how to behave. If your memories belong to the night, wreckage is possible. Yet, some nocturnal animals, like porcupine, see in the dark, eat plywood glue and bark. Their quills are fire spears. I didn't have to decide if I was staying or just passing through. I'd already married the circle of cold to my bones.

LEAVING FOR THE UNIVERSITY

Clock hands
that walked slow for months,
today resume a normal rhythm.
Looking back toward home
I mouth goodbyes
to the wild trees
busy at their daily work.

Half a moon hangs pewter over Flattop,
the driveway's tapestry
of orange leaves and brown birds
scatter as our car passes.
I carry my history stitched into my skin.

Tucked in a blue suitcase
is a turquoise sweater,
silver transistor radio,
and things I learn later
to leave by the road.

WHOLE

Red flowers poke up
like sleepwalkers

along the gray strip of asphalt.

I steer down the highway
past boarded-up buildings.

Driving without music,

remembering
my brother and sister,

the three of us suspended
on a hand-hewn footbridge,

young, still pretending at our lives.

On either side of us
a tangle of spring alders,

their bruise of gray stems
like arms of lovers
we shouldn't have mixed with.

We were whole and fine,

and the sun rose
thick and orange,

painting our arms,
our open faces.

HER GARDEN

Mid-July her transplants still in pots,
crabgrass, thistle, wild morning glory
choke her raised beds. This story
familiar—a rainy May, her plot

too wet to plant. I kneel to weed
and set her calendar back to spring.
I wear gloves, but she weeds
barehanded, soil between her fingers,
her wrists exposed.

The sting of small cuts is nothing
when stains of past bruises linger
on her skin. As children, we played
with dump trucks, cut paper dolls

from catalogs, how enthralled
we were with life, until she was abused.
Who was listening then
or later as she took up with useless men?

Overgrown by years, we don't discuss
these things. I dig out all the big weeds.
It's then I feel like I am saving
her life. We mark the rows with string
plant tomatoes, broccoli, her seeds.

MAY, AT MY FATHER'S BURIAL

The coffin lowered now,
covered over by earth.
All the while, the wind

runs its cold, melancholy hands
through my hair.
We are out of time.

No more chances
he might speak to me from his heart.
Grief and loss are cousins now—

figures caught this day of sorrow
looking in the mirror at my blue reflection.
I shiver and draw death's sad robe

around my shoulders.
I am not the first to wear it,
but that's a lonely comfort.

Then a flock of white homing pigeons,
released by friends, circles the mourners.
Their bright bodies wheel

against the overcast sky,
gaining altitude with each revolution.
The thump and whir of their wings

like an ancient drum,
until at last they climb the sky,
casting off for home.

TO DUST

I tuck the cardboard box
in the trunk of my car.
        Inside, not the gray sand
of Seldovia's beach,
        or the fallen stars of dreams,
but her seared bones crumbled to ash.

Driving alone to the place we both loved,
I recite the litany of her life,
        how empty it was,
how empty she let it be—
        the pavement is hard
like the sadness that hollowed her.

When she was alive
I brought her red cranberries
        she made into sauce,
bouquets of wildflowers,
        intoxicating as her liquor.

Even now above our ruined place,
the Chugach peaks shrouded by clouds,
        the trees cloaked in green froth
like it always was in spring.

I look toward my sister and brother,
glad they have come.
        We make baskets of our hands,
take the ash,
these fragments, all that is left—

throw them on Dad's grave,
and in the street covering our driveway,
        on the clump of trees
that grew near the homestead's garage.

Into the yards of strangers
who live here now,
        but do not come out of their duplexes.
Our skin is like the bark of the missing trees.

Raised on solitude,
everything I knew
learned on our homestead
picking blueberries from scattered bushes,
their citrus and sweet juice
spreading on my tongue.
By the creek,
kneeling to catch tadpoles
carried home in jam jars—
at the moose swamp's edge
where Dad perched in a tree
waiting for the winter meat.
Not in the Baptist pew
he and his new wife favored
after the divorce,
where he was saved,
in case there's a heaven.

Back from college, his talking,
interrupting my story of black scoters
migrating along the Bering Sea coast,
the shrill whistling of their wings,
their calls a hoarse *kraaaa.*
How they blanketed the sky
like a resurrection—
a different resurrection than his.
That afternoon in our kitchen
when Dad said
he left the homestead to us kids,
sun came through the blinds,
broke apart, shredded into ribbons.
His confident voice,

his words so sure.
I wanted to believe him.

But my stepmother
changed the will after he died
knowing the dead
would never know
she wiped out our names.
I discovered
how easy it is to become irrelevant,
how quickly I bruise.
By then I'd forgotten how to pray,
so I sat by the river,
let go of pretending to love her,
watched lost trees slide through the water,
and dark branches of spruce bend
from their trunks to the forest floor,
all the light sucked out of them.

The earth near our place
        was cradle,
it rocked us—
        became our skin.
House doors opened,
        spilled us out,
we disappeared into trees—
        they clothed us
in delirious green.
We wore them like coats,
        learned from black branches
and bent trunks
        their sun and rain
vocabulary.
        We grew up astonished, whole,
but ghosts of ourselves,
        shushed, mourned by wind.
Our tongues tasted sun, our shoes
        muddy, scouting creek.
We chewed dogwood berries,
        learned later they were poisonous,
lay in tall grass
        as clouds revealed their animals.
Saw iris petals
        like purple flags—
walked to cranberries,
        picked some, scarlet like lips.
Claustrophobic walls
        exchanged for this—
light and shadow,
        everything unresolved, lonely.

We knew the song
        of this place, made it up,
sang it—
        not a lament
until years later.

ACKNOWLEDGMENTS

I am sincerely grateful to the Rasmuson Foundation for an Individual
Artist Project Award that allowed me time to work on this book.

Thanks to the editors of the following journals where these poems
previously appeared, sometimes in greatly different versions:

> *Alaska Women Speak*: "Stealing the Strawberries"
> *Cirque*: "Today Is All They Have," "No One Asks about the Bridge"
> *Connecticut River Review*: "In the Playhouse"
> *Ice-Floe*: "I Watch the Hired Men Pick Potatoes"
> *Permafrost*: "The Winter Meat"
> *The Fairbanks Daily News-Miner*: "Sleeping the Chickens,"
>   "May, at My Father's Burial," "Neighbors"
> *The Northern Review*: "Mountains Like Ribs" (published as
>   "Along the Road to Seward"), "Along the Print," "Coming Out
>   of Nowhere"
> *Tiny Moments Anthology*: "Summer Untethered"

This book wouldn't have been possible without the support of many
other people, including members of my writing group: Jean Anderson,
Susan Campbell, Marjorie Cole, Burns Cooper, Cindy Hardy, Shanna
Karella, Susheila Khera, John Kooistra, and John Morgan. Their careful
reading and insightful comments were invaluable. John Kooistra also
critically read drafts of most of the poems in the manuscript. Longtime
friends Elyse Guttenberg, William Schneider, Jean Anderson, and Dan
O'Neill offered support and wise advice as this manuscript developed.
Finally, to the University of Alaska Press community, especially Nate
Bauer, director and acquisitions editor, for believing in this book.

Stephen Sparks at Quantum Spatial tracked down the 1950 aerial pho-
tograph of the homestead house, garage, and woodshed and the 2008
aerial photo of the same area. He also shared copies of old Anchorage
maps. I am thankful for his time, interest, and generosity.

I am greatly indebted to Chris and Tony Pastro for sharing their family
photographs that were taken at the homestead in the late forties and
early fifties.

p. ix. Campbell Creek Trail, which branched off: US Bureau of Land Management, *Land Ownership Map, Anchorage Area, Alaska*, December 1946, and other maps of that epoch, obtained from the Anchorage Museum, by Steven Sparks, Quantum Spatial, Anchorage, Alaska.

p. ix. The homestead legal description: Information taken from US Land Patent Number 1132237, granted to John Daniel Schandelmeier, June 6, 1951.

p. ix. The Seward Highway (now called the Old Seward Highway): John D. Schandelmeier, personal communication.

p. ix. When the road was originally built: Nell Schandelmeier, personal communication; *Anchorage and Vicinity Map*, copyright 1951, by D. M. Stone, Anchorage Alaska.

p. x. The 1950 Census: http://live.laborstats.alaska.gov/cen/hist.cfm

p. x. To acquire title to their land: "About the Homestead Act," National Park Service, last updated April 10, 2015, https://www.nps.gov/home/learn/historyculture/abouthomesteadactlaw.htm.

p. xiii. The way of poets, as Emily Dickinson described: *The Complete Poems of Emily Dickinson*, edited by Thomas H. Johnson (Boston: Little, Brown and Company, 1960), 506.

Former homestead house

Alaska Railroad

Old Seward Highway

O'Malley Road

A 2008 aerial photo of the homestead site south of Anchorage. When compared to the 1950 photo of the same location on p. ii., much new development is evident. (Photo © Quantum Spatial)